Explaining Rejection

Steve Hepden

D1354099

Sovereign World

Sovereign World Ltd
PO Box 777
Tonbridge
Kent TN11 0ZS
England

ISBN 1 85240 336 5

The publishers aim to produce books which will help to extend and build
up the Kingdom of God. We do not necessarily agree with every view
expressed by the author, or with every interpretation of Scripture expressed.
We expect each reader to make their judgment in the light of their own
understanding of God's Word and in an attitude of Christian love and
fellowship.

Cover design by CCD, www.ccdgroup.co.uk
Typeset by CRB Associates, Reepham, Norfolk
Printed in the United States of America

Contents

Acknowledgements

To Chris, without whom it would never have happened,
who in the midst of her own suffering let me go
to fulfill God's purposes;

To my daughters Joanna and Zoe,
who have been so caring and patient with their dad;

To the many people who over the years
have given themselves to be counseled by me;

Also to my friends in leadership
who have trusted and released me
to pray for many hurt and afflicted people.

1

Understanding rejection

The little girl was standing on her own in the railway station of the big city. Her parents had been fighting with each other and had finally gone their separate ways. Neither of them were prepared to take their three-year-old daughter and so they left her alone at the station.

Ann had become an orphan, although both of her parents were alive. She was taken into care and stayed until her teenage years in a well-known orphanage. Can you imagine what went on in that child's heart?

There was nothing hidden about her rejection – it was open and obvious. She wasn't wanted;, she wasn't loved, she was thrown away like rubbish. Many say that children are too young to really understand and be affected by rejection. Yet our experience tells otherwise.

Ann grew up with a desperate hunger to be loved and cared for. As a teenager she grabbed for anything that would satisfy her inner longing for acceptance. Her boyfriend would creep into the orphanage at night up the fire escape, sleep with her, and then get out quickly before matron did her early morning visits.

Tony had six sisters, five of them from different fathers, some of them of different races. Which man was his father? Imagine the confusion, the rejection and the hurt that came through the different men. Tony was emotionally crippled by insecurity and self-rejection. He was naturally sensitive, but in a way that made him unable to handle deep relationships.

Years later, Ann and Tony each became Christians. They both joined the same church fellowship in their home town. After a very special meeting where the Holy Spirit moved in great power, we prayed for Ann and Tony. As the issue of rejection came up for Tony, Ann began to react severely. The same happened as we prayed for Ann – Tony was deeply affected. It took time, but it was amazing to see the Holy Spirit begin to deliver them both at the same time!

Tony and Ann fell in love with each other and got married. They now have a daughter whom they love dearly. There is no rejection – it has gone. They are more secure than ever before in their lives. Out of their childhood hurts, wounds and bondages of rejection they have found the love of God and acceptance in each other.

What is rejection?

Rejection is very often linked back to childhood. It can come from a significant person's refusal to acknowledge or accept us. It can result from being forsaken or abandoned, from being discarded as useless, unsatisfactory, or worthless. Feelings of rejection often arise from not being loved as we are, but feeling that we need to constantly act a part.

We all need and crave love – it's the way God has made us. In an atmosphere of love, acceptance, and approval we can grow into a sense of security and well-being.

The existence of rejection does not necessarily mean that there is no love at all in the home. Often parents are caring, but because they themselves have not received all that they needed in childhood, they are unable to express affection, touch, or the spoken word that builds up or affirms. If these things are absent, the symptoms of rejection will flood in uninvited to fill the void.

Rejection causes deep wounds in the inward self, which may be revealed by abnormal behavioral patterns and attitudes. Often the hurting person will suffer a loss of identity, leading to withdrawal, defensive attitudes, or rebellion. They may be desperately asking the questions, "Who am I?", "Where am I going?" and "What is my role?"

Such wounds require emotional healing through prayer and counseling, healing that is available through the Lord Jesus.

The feelings of rejection

It is easier to experience rejection than to explain it or understand it! Many people feel unloved or unwanted, which is often coupled with a sense of being worthless. This leads to feelings of inadequacy, inferiority and insecurity. "Everyone is better than me or does things better than me. I don't feel secure in who I am. I have no identity, no real role in life."

For many, guilt enters the picture. This can lead to strong self-rejection and a tendency to continually speak negative words to oneself. "I've never liked myself. I can't change. If only I was like that other person ... " Many destructive ideas can be entertained.

The person who feels rejected cannot accept love, spoken affirmation or physical expressions of affection. Self-protective barriers go up because of the fear of unbearable further rejection. No one is allowed close.

Rejection affects all relationships

How can a person who feels totally rejected accept the love of God? It is not easy. They find it difficult enough even getting close to other people. Feelings of rejection often occur with very little apparent cause. It becomes more comfortable to keep the barriers up and refuse to let others in.

Sometimes people cannot give love because they have not received love themselves, and they can't understand it. You can't receive what you don't recognize. You can't give what you don't possess yourself. So it's easy to retreat, and rejection grows a little more.

Rejection can affect every area of a person's life, deeply wounding the inner personality and spirit. It can begin at any time, although it is most commonly rooted in childhood or even the womb. Although it may not be seen as such in those early years, rejection is like a seed that takes root in a certain kind of soil, and perhaps manifests later. A trauma or negative circumstance can trigger and release it, and then another layer of rejection forms.

It has been said that rejection is the greatest undiagnosed, and therefore untreated illness in the body of Christ today. If that is true, as I believe it is, how are we dealing with it in the church, and what about people outside the body of Christ?

2

Why rejection is a problem

Mephibosheth was one of the many rejected people mentioned in the Bible. 2 Samuel 4:4 records the childhood event that affected the rest of his life. When he was five years old, the news came that his father Jonathan and grandfather Saul had been killed in battle. His frightened nurse picked him up to flee, but Mephibosheth fell (or perhaps was dropped) and he was crippled in both feet.

Names in the Old Testament can give insight into the personality or destiny of the person who possesses them. Mephibosheth's name means in Hebrew, *"from the mouth of the shameful thing."* He was not only crippled physically at an early age, but was also crippled inside. The deaths of his father and grandfather were a great loss. (It is common for a child to feel rejected by someone who leaves them, even by death.)

Mephibosheth was also left with a physical deformity which would isolate him from others and cause feelings of self-rejection, inadequacy and inferiority. His family's defeat meant the loss of his royal inheritance. He grew up a physically and emotionally broken man, in a place called Lo Debar, which itself means *"barrenness, infertile, no pasture."*

I know many modern-day Mephibosheths, affected by roots of rejection, crippled within by shame and living in barren places. Rejection which begins at a very early age often becomes an inseparable part of the person, stunting their growth in every way.

We read the sequel to this story in 2 Samuel 9:1–13. Years later, King David remembered his covenant of friendship with Jonathan and asked if there was anyone left in that family whom he could help. An old servant of Saul called Ziba mentioned Mephibosheth and the king sent for him. When the two men met, David promised to show kindness to Mephibosheth and restore the land of his father and grandfather. From then on, he would eat at the king's table as an honored guest.

Mephibosheth's answer is revealing: *"What is your servant, that you should notice a dead dog like me?"* His self-denigrating words reflected the sense of worthlessness that he felt inside. Yet the king spoke words of restoration and reconciliation, restoring to Mephibosheth and his offspring their lost inheritance.

We see in this a picture of how our king Jesus desires to bring healing to us. He calls us to sit and eat at his table and he restores to us what we have lost. Psalm 23:5 expresses it so well:

You prepare a table for me
* in the presence of my enemies.*
You anoint my head with oil;
* my cup overflows.*

We want this overflowing cup, and we want God's anointing. But unless we deal with roots of rejection within us, they can prevent us from sitting at the table to commune with God.

Rejection affects the whole person

The story of Mephibosheth shows how rejection is not just a slight and short-lived problem. It is something that can affect us for the whole of our lives. It can also affect our entire selves, spirit, soul and body.

Spirit

When God created Adam from the dust of the ground, he breathed his life into him so that Adam became a living being. This breath – or spirit – is the unique gift of God. It is the capacity within us to encounter God, become conscious of him and experience his presence.

The Bible is very clear that this area of our being can be affected negatively. Proverbs 18:14 says,

> *One's spirit provides strength in times of sickness,*
> *but a crushed spirit who can bear?*

Wounds coming through the circumstances and traumas of life can affect every part of us, even our spirits. Because of this it is not surprising that so many rejected people have difficulty in their relationship with God.

The enemy plays a part, by oppressing our spirits. Jesus said that the devil comes to *"steal and kill and destroy"* (John 10:10). Some people can have a "spirit of rejection" which needs to be overcome by the authority of Christ.

Soul

Rejection will certainly affect our soul. This includes our will, intellect, and emotions. This means that the ability to make right decisions and choices about the way we behave can be compromised by our reaction to past rejection. Besides this, a sense of rejection can affect our memories and hinder our capacity to think and reason. Finally, it can affect our emotions, either to the extent that we seem to have no feelings, or that we cannot control our feelings.

When we are told that we are no good again and again, it alters us on the inside. Our own emotions begin to tell us the same thing; and our outward behavior gives the same message to other people. The message of rejection is reinforced again and again.

Body

We need to thank God for our bodies. We also need to be responsible in the way we treat them. Some people experience rejection because they have been told constantly that they are ugly, or made fun of because of physical problems. Many people believe they are the wrong shape: too big, too small, too thin, too fat, too long a nose, etc. Self-rejection, focused on the physical body, can quickly take over. It may well affect our health, our posture, and the way we look.

Identity and image

God has made us as individuals with unique personalities. We are all different and all important in God's plan. In the beginning God said,

> *Let us make human beings in our image, in our likeness.*
> (Genesis 1:26)

As men and women we reflect God's likeness. We were created to represent the reality of who he is.

Self-image is the way we see ourselves. It is a map, drawn according to our self-beliefs, which we consult about ourselves. When we become Christians, the Holy Spirit makes us alive to God. If our self-image is unhealthy (the map is wrong), there will be a conflict between the way we see ourselves and the way we know God sees us.

Our self-image can be affected by different sources. In our early years we totally depend on the reactions around us to arrive at an understanding of who we are. A newborn baby is completely open and impressionable. The growing child's perception of life is filtered through the words, attitudes, and behavior of its parents and other significant figures. As we looked through this childhood mirror, what reflection did we see? The distortions then are never forgotten.

From childhood we also pick up many of the world's ideas. These can affect the way we see ourselves, positively or negatively. Our individual makeup can also influence the way we feel and respond to particular circumstances. Moreover, Satan is the accuser, the one who whispers words of condemnation and guilt. He is the father of lies and tries to stop us believing that God actually accepts us.

When Jesus was asked what the greatest commandment was, he summed it up very clearly:

"Love the Lord your God with all your heart and with all your soul and with all your mind." This is the first and greatest commandment. And the second is like it: "Love your neighbor as yourself." (Matthew 22:36–39)

How can we love God and our neighbor if we cannot even accept or love ourselves?

We have an inbuilt need for recognition and acceptance. Jesus fulfilled this, and enabled us to have peace with God and with ourselves. Yet we may have been conditioned by our environment to believe that we can only gain acceptance by behaving in a certain way.

When we fear rejection, we tend to wear "masks" so that we don't have to reveal the real person underneath. We behave differently depending on who we are with. We hide our true feelings, constructing an unreal image to impress others. If we have experienced rejection, we think that our identity is in what we do. God tells us that our identity is in what we are!

God sent his Son – the very stamp of God's nature and being – to restore and redeem us. Yet often rejection has such a deep root in us that we cannot accept this. We still feel worthless, useless, inferior and inadequate.

Proverbs 27:19 says,

As water reflects your face,
so your heart reflects you.

Rejection will make us think and act in a way that is almost the opposite to what we know the Christian life to be.

Questions

1. How do you respond when you look in a mirror? Do you feel good?

2. Are you important in God's plan? Do you feel needed and of value in the Kingdom?

3. Do people really love you? Do you have a healthy sense of belonging? Are you aware of being wanted, accepted, cared for and enjoyed?

4. Do you feel that you have the ability to get through life? Can you cope competently with situations that arise?

5. Can you move freely as the person God created you to be? Or are you locked up in yourself, feeling condemned and guilty?

Can demons be a source of rejection?

Rejection violates the very character and heart of a person. It quickly bruises the spirit. It will also affect a person's mind, hindering them from making decisions and experiencing normal emotion.

My experience of counseling shows clearly that demonic powers will enter through these wounds and feed on them. We can't be sentimental: evil spirits do not respect vulnerable people and they can cause damage even from the womb. Evil spirits must have an open door to enter a person, and rejection can become that door to affliction and oppression.

In some cases rejection can have ancestral roots. It is quite possible for children to inherit wounds and demonic influences linked to rejection. Many times in counseling I have found the source of rejection in past generations, living or dead. The Lord said to Moses that he punishes children and grandchildren for the sin of the parents (Exodus 34:7).

Hurts wound, while bondages bind. Often demons become attached to emotional wounds, ultimately causing bondage. People may need both the healing of their wounds and the breaking of demonic bondages. We need to discern, asking the Holy Spirit for guidance.

Many Christians believe they can't be affected by demons. Yet when we became Christians, did we permanently stop sinning or getting ill? No. We are taught to possess the land and overcome in the name of Jesus. But we sometimes fail. In some cases, demonic powers have come in before the person was born again. It is actually the power of the Holy Spirit within and the Christian's choice to grow in God which has exposed the demonic.

It is true that the word demon "possession" is not entirely

right, though it is used in some translations. Possession means ownership, and Christians have deliberately submitted to the ownership and lordship of Jesus Christ, not any demonic power. A demon cannot invade and indwell a person's spirit if the Holy Spirit is there. But as we have seen, demons can hinder or block Christians in their spiritual life.

A better translation is "to have a spirit," or to be "demonized." Another biblical term denotes bondage or slavery to the demon. There are certain types of evil spirits specifically related to rejection, often entering through some sort of trauma. Because we are undiscerning, problems go unrecognized for years. Yet each time there is a trigger event, rejection rears its ugly head.

Is rejection easy to cure?

Basically, no! Rejection causes major problems with multitudes of people whether they are Christians or not. It is essential that we do not rush to solve a problem too quickly, when that person has been hurting for many years.

Rejection is part of the curse on humankind. We need to face it realistically, knowing that discernment, patience, mercy, understanding and authority are all required. Often discipleship or mentoring can be part of the follow-up work. Without knowledge of the Holy Spirit, we are lost – we must listen to him and trust him to lead us.

3

The spiritual source of rejection

To understand the nature of rejection, we need to look at its origins. Often people are unaware that their problems are sourced in rejection because they only look at the fruit and go no further.

You may be surprised to know that the source of rejection is in the very beginning of humanity, with Adam and Eve and their sons, Cain and Abel. It seems that rejection has been around as long as human beings!

The core issue is not roots – which we will look at later – but source. In order for roots to grow, a seed must be planted in a certain kind of ground. It is this ground that is the source of the rejection that plagues us.

The garden

The Garden of Eden was created by God as a place of harmony and complete relationships. In it Adam and Eve could commune together, communicating freely with each other and with their Maker. They would often hear the sound of God walking in the garden and they were at one with him.

Genesis 1:31 sums it up:

God saw all that he had made and it was very good.

Not just good, but very good! Both the man and the woman were totally affirmed and accepted in their identity, and secure in their roles. As they lived in the garden they had a true sense of worth and belonging.

It was in this garden that God gave the man and woman a commission which was to last forever. Genesis 1:28 says that,

> *God blessed them and said to them, "Be fruitful and increase in number; fill the earth and subdue it. Rule over ... every living creature."*

So from the beginning God told them to be fruitful sexually, and to take authority spiritually. This was to be their truest calling and capacity. God gave them everything they needed to live fulfilled and satisfied on this earth.

The enemy

It was in this ideal environment that Satan came to tempt Adam and Eve. He hit at the heart of the issue by challenging their willingness to submit to God. Satan claimed about the forbidden fruit,

> *God knows that when you eat of it your eyes will be opened, and you will be like God, knowing good and evil.*   (Genesis 3:5)

In this one event Satan undermined God's word, gave Adam and Eve false expectations and distorted their image of God and of themselves. They had to make a choice about whether or not they would continue to obey God's commands.

God gave human beings free will, the right and responsibility to make choices. They chose to believe the serpent instead of their Creator. In rebelling against God, Adam and Eve rejected him.

The curse

Usually when God came into the garden, there was happy fellowship. But after the man and woman rejected God, they hid in fear and shame. Neither would take responsibility for their sin: the man blamed the woman, and the woman blamed the devil (Genesis 3:11–13).

Yet they were all accountable, because they had chosen to turn away from God and disobey him. Because of this, they lost their spiritual, mental, emotional and physical harmony with each other and with God. Instead of innocence there was shame; instead of relationship, there was division.

Because of their rejection of God, he ejected Adam and Eve from the garden. Their disobedience became a curse to them as they were exiled to a fallen world. They could not return: death had set in. At that point, rejection took root for them and their offspring, and through them the whole of the human race.

The sons

After the fall, Adam and Eve were isolated and damaged. Even the animals and the land seemed against them. Into this fallen world their sons Cain and Abel were born.

It seems that something of the rejection of the parents passed to Cain, their firstborn. Throughout Scripture the firstborn has significance: Abel offered the firstborn of his flock to God (Genesis 4:4); first fruits of the harvest were a special offering to God (Deuteronomy 26:1–4), and God calls Israel his firstborn son (Exodus 4:23). Perhaps because Satan was aware of the special nature of the firstborn he wanted to destroy it right from the beginning.

In any case there is a generational link with the sins of the parents. The opening that Adam and Eve gave to the devil was also a blight on their children. It seems unfair, yet Cain still had a choice about sin.

The offerings

Genesis 4:2–5 tells us that Abel kept flocks and Cain worked the soil. They each brought some of the fruits of their labor as an offering to God, but only Abel's was accepted. Hebrews 11:4 tells us,

By faith Abel offered God a better sacrifice than Cain did. By faith he was commended as righteous, when God spoke well of his offerings. And by faith he still speaks, even though he is dead.

Abel's offering was by faith – a pure response to God. By contrast, it would seem, Cain's offering was to do with works – to get acceptance and affirmation for himself. Scripture indicates that his motives were impure. 1 John 3:12 says,

Do not be like Cain, who belonged to the evil one and murdered his brother. And why did he murder him? Because his own actions were evil and his brother's were righteous.

The reaction

Genesis tells us that Cain was very angry, and his face was downcast. There was a mixture of resentment and self-pity which moved into rebellion. Yet God came in grace and compassion to reason with Cain. He asked why Cain was so angry and upset, and said, *"If you do what is right, will you not be accepted?"* (Genesis 4:7).

God was giving Cain another opportunity to get it right. Yet Cain wanted it right his way, not God's. So often we have to make the choice of responding to God. Obedience will mean acceptance, but disobedience will mean rejection.

The warning

God then gave the critical warning to Cain:

But if you will not do what is right, sin is crouching at your door; it desires to have you, but you must master it.   (Genesis 4:7)

This is a prophetic warning of what was happening in the spiritual realm – the enemy was lying in wait at his door, ready at any moment to come in.

God was letting Cain know the seriousness of his situation, and telling him what choice he had to make. We can never put all the blame on our personal hurts or on the devil: we still have personal responsibility. God says Cain must master, or overcome, the sin lurking inside him. He wouldn't say that unless it was actually possible to overcome, by his grace!

The judgment

Tragically, Cain chose to ignore God's words. He enticed Abel into a field and killed him (Genesis 4:8), releasing all of his hatred and anger onto his own brother. When God asked him what had happened, he lied, saying he did not know, and then asked defiantly, *"Am I my brother's keeper?"*

The result was a curse. In rejecting God and his ways, Cain became his own victim, and was rejected by God. He became a marked man and was driven to be a restless wanderer throughout the earth.

In Genesis 4:13–14, Cain says to God, *"My punishment is more than I can bear."* He is filled with anguish and paranoia – a fear of persecution and death. *"I will be hidden from your presence ... and whoever finds me will kill me."*

This is a very significant picture of rejection. Because rejection is tied up with identity and image, many rejected people never find fulfillment in who they are. They are always driven to look for something more, something they can never find. This restlessness means they can never find satisfaction, continually reinforcing their sense of rejection.

Summary

These early passages from Genesis show us the source and roots of rejection. It is clear that rejection has been a curse on humankind from the very first family. We also see that it can be hereditary, passing down through the generations.

It is also clear that Satan and his demonic powers have a significant part to play in rejection. Nevertheless we have free will to choose good or evil, and never can absolve ourselves of personal responsibility. Scripture entreats us, *"Do not be like Cain"* (1 John 3:12) and judges those who have *"taken the way of Cain"* (Jude 11). It is a serious message to us all.

4

The roots of rejection

When a seed has been planted and the conditions are right, it is not long before the roots begin to grow. Roots are normally the hidden parts of the plant, yet they are vital to the whole. The roots of a tree anchor and support it, and are a source of nourishment. They may be as deep in the ground as the tree is tall – anyone who has tried to dig out the roots of a large tree will understand how difficult and lengthy a job it is.

We cannot disregard the roots of rejection. They are often deep and strong, have developed for many years, and need careful and sensitive handling when they become exposed, ready to cut off.

It is fairly straightforward to deal with fruit in a person's life, just as it is easy to pick the fruit off a tree. Yet if the roots are not dealt with, the negative fruit of sin will return again and again and cause frustration. The Lord said of the sin of the Amorites,

> *I destroyed their fruit above*
> *and their roots below.* (Amos 2:9)

It is vital to identify and deal with the roots of rejection.

Three different roots

Although there are many fruits of rejection, and many causes, there seem to be only three basic roots.

25

Rebellion

Rebelliousness is an aggressive reaction to rejection, and shows itself as opposition or defiance. When a rejected person reacts this way, anyone who gets in their way can be affected. Anger, arrogance or criticism may be openly displayed. Often these emotions are deeply hidden but will erupt like a volcano when provoked, injuring the person and those around them.

There is a definite link between rebellion and witchcraft. Samuel said to Saul,

> *For rebellion is like the sin of divination or witchcraft,*
> * and stubbornness or arrogance is like iniquity and idolatry.*
> *Because you have rejected the word of the Lord,*
> * he has rejected you as king.*   (1 Samuel 15:23)

Remember Cain? Often evil spirits are behind rebellion and control, greatly increasing the problem.

Self-rejection

Many people take rejection into their own self and begin to reject and hurt themselves. This can be through self-hatred, cursing themselves, or being physically violent to their own bodies. This can be terribly destructive and even lead to suicide.

There is a sick self-orientation in this reaction. The roots of rejection keep growing while being fed by self-rejecting thoughts, words, and actions. It is not difficult to turn the thoughts of rejection inward, and many of those who do so think of it as less sinful than outwardly-directed aggression. Yet when we reject ourselves, we will finally reject the God who made us.

Self-protection

Self-protection is caused by fear of rejection. Fear is always around the corner when rejection affects a person. The fear of additional hurt will create defensive barriers that are hard to dismantle, and which create major barriers to relating to others.

Many rejected people ask themselves, "Can I trust anyone? Will I be hurt again?" They close off inner feelings, taking control so that no one can get close enough to cause the same damage. Some people become seemingly emotionless because their defensive barriers are so impregnable.

Different reactions

Rejection can affect any person, whatever their character or personality. Because different people react differently, there can be manifestations of any of the three roots. It is not uncommon for all three to be involved. The mind, will and emotions can all be influenced, causing attitude and behavior change.

One man that I counseled felt unable to respond to God as Father, and his emotions were completely locked up. He had experienced rejection in early childhood which had left a strong reaction of anger and hate (rebellion), deep insecurity, inadequacy and inferiority (self-rejection) as well as criticism and pride, fear of failure and domination (self-protection). The outward reaction was his expressions of anger and hate. The inward reaction was the way his deep hurts had blocked off early memories and prevented him from weeping.

These roots can be demonic. There are actually demons called "rebellion," "self-rejection" and "self-protection," and even simply called "rejection." We need to learn to discern between demons and wounds, and to know when both are present.

One demonic power called the "orphan spirit" is clearly linked to lack of love, care, affectionate touch, security and right discipline in a person's early months or years. Ultimately a spirit may seek to oppress such a person. They have a sense of being orphaned or abandoned regardless of whether the parents are actually living, and are resistant to receiving love from others. People affected by this spirit find it hard to respond to the Father-heart of God. How can they when they haven't received love from their earthly parents?

Control is another issue closely linked with rejection. It is a conscious or unconscious power over another person that manifests as domination, superiority or emotional manipulation. This can be driven by a reaction to rejection in the past.

There is also a link between wrongful control and witchcraft. The Holy Spirit will be grieved by inappropriate domination and manipulation, and strong occult spirits can come in.

Suppression of emotions and memories can also be a form of control related to rejection. The dam that is created is a hard and harsh reaction covering up much hurt. If a spirit of control comes in behind it, a bondage will be created. I have known many people who come to faith afflicted with this kind of control and are unable to release their emotions, worship freely or be open to the moving of the Holy Spirit. It is vital to discern these roots so that they can be released.

A more outward form of control is domination. Rejected people have a fear of domination or further rejection, and will try to control a situation or person to make sure this does not happen. They may do this by conditional love – threatening to withdraw love unless a person submits to their control. Because children are very dependent, they are especially vulnerable to wrong forms of control. One example is the "Jezebel" spirit, referred to in Revelation 2:20–22, which involves false teaching or prophecy, sexual immorality, and strange religious practices.

I believe there is a demon called the "spirit of the little boy" or the "spirit of the little girl." Often a child rejected and traumatized in the early years is stunted in their emotional growth, and a demonic bondage may also be present. I have met many adults who are in part still little boys or little girls and react with inappropriate emotion to certain situations. Of course the emotions need releasing and healing, while the demonic powers must also be dealt with. Great sensitivity is needed!

5

The fruit of rejection

Fruit can be defined as the product or result of something. As a seed is sown, it will root into the ground, send up a shoot, and when it is mature will produce a seed-bearing body. Usually fruits are above ground, and sometimes they are edible.

Rejection produces its own distinctive fruit. It is often easy to identify it and deal with it without touching the root, but then the fruit is liable to return. That is why I have first emphasized dealing with the root.

The fruit of rejection may manifest in either outward, visible behaviors or hidden, inward ways. It is important to understand them so that the roots may also be recognized.

In an outward, visible reaction, people can be over-emotional, loudly expressing anger, or being aggressive or overbearing. Rejected people sometimes defend themselves by attacking others. Because of their fear of being hurt, they put up defensive barriers, while at the same time reacting strongly to others.

In an internal, hidden reaction, there may be suppression of emotions like a dam. Long-hidden memories are still affecting the person. Rejected people often escape into themselves, because it is easier to hide than to cope with reality. There may be a reluctance to communicate honestly, so the real person is not seen.

Whether outward or inward, the response is unconsciously motivated. In other words, people do not know why they react as they do, and why they are having problems in everyday life. This will affect their sense of identity and basic role in life.

Symptoms of rejection

The fruit of rejection is revealed in different signs and symptoms. If we can be informed about their meaning and relate them to our own personalities, a picture will be built up that will help to identify the roots of rejection.

One example of a character weakness is insecurity – lacking confidence in situations, being unsure or unstable. Linked with other key symptoms it will highlight the possibility of a root of self-rejection.

I often use the following words as a diagnostic test for people whom I suspect have a root of rejection. Each word is defined to help explain the meaning. I go quickly through the list, asking the person to mark themselves honestly on a scale of 1 to 5 according to how closely the word applies to them: 1 would mean the word does not apply at all, and 5 would mean it very definitely does.

You can go as far back over the years as memory allows. It may help to involve someone close to the person or their spouse, in order to get their opinion or confirmation. Remember to be discerning and sensitive to the Holy Spirit. Whether the fruits are fleshly reactions or actually demonic, discipleship will be necessary in follow-up.

As the marks are added up in the word groupings, a high score in one section indicates the presence of that specific root.

Fruit relating to rebellion

► Harshness; severe or rough language
► Rejection of others (often when the person is under pressure in relationships)
► Hardness: unyielding and impenetrable attitudes
► Unbelief: refusal or inability to believe
► Skepticism: strong doubt or undermining attitude
► Defiance: hostility, resistance, disobedience
► Arrogance: feeling of superiority shown in an overbearing attitude

- ▶ Stubbornness: unwillingness to give way in situations
- ▶ Anger: rage, fits of temper, or smoldering anger
- ▶ Violence: destructive words or actions
- ▶ Bitterness: deep-rooted resentment and poisoned attitudes
- ▶ Addiction: use of drugs or other substances to remove emotional pain
- ▶ Occultism: witchcraft, divination, New Age practices, idolatry
- ▶ Legalism: exalting law over grace
- ▶ Lust: excessive, self-centered desire for power, sex, money, etc.
- ▶ Control: domination or manipulation of others
- ▶ Aggression: pushy and offensive behavior
- ▶ Refusing to receive affection: will not receive comfort from others
- ▶ Argumentativeness: given to quarrels and disputes
- ▶ Vengefulness: tendency to retaliate verbally or physically.

Fruit relating to self-rejection

- ▶ Low self-image: the belief "I am worthless"
- ▶ Inferiority: the sense of being lower than everyone else
- ▶ Inadequacy: inability to cope with tasks; the words "I can't"
- ▶ Sadness: intense unhappiness, dejection, depression
- ▶ Grief: heartache and anguish due to loss
- ▶ Shame: disgrace, humiliation related to one's behavior
- ▶ Self-accusation: constant sense of guilt or being wrong
- ▶ Self-condemnation: sense of needing to be punished, inability to accept praise
- ▶ Inability to communicate
- ▶ Fear of failure; panic attacks
- ▶ Insecurity: lack of confidence
- ▶ Disappointment: constant sense of unfulfilled desires

- ▶ Loneliness: isolation and pain of being alone
- ▶ Hopelessness: despair, sense of "no way out"
- ▶ Wrong expectations: inappropriate assumptions
- ▶ Seeking to please: need to find favor with everyone
- ▶ Anxiety: worry, fretfulness, apprehension
- ▶ Infirmity: sickness or physical disability brought on by self-rejection.

Fruit relating to self-protection

- ▶ Pressure to perform: "I must be competent to gain acceptance"
- ▶ Pressure to achieve: "I must be successful in everything"
- ▶ Striving: trying too hard, strenuous effort that causes inner conflict
- ▶ Restlessness: drivenness, inability to settle or find contentment
- ▶ Competitiveness: "I must be superior to everyone else"
- ▶ Independence: "I can do without you, I will do everything myself"
- ▶ Self-centeredness: "I'm only interested in myself"
- ▶ Self-justification: always seeking to excuse oneself
- ▶ Self-righteousness: always right, never wrong in own eyes
- ▶ Criticism: constantly finding fault, disapproving, undermining
- ▶ Judgmentalism: authoritatively hostile attitudes towards others
- ▶ Jealousy: suspicion of others who have what you want
- ▶ Envy: intense desire to have what another has
- ▶ Self-pity: sulking, constantly sorry for oneself
- ▶ Pride: overly high opinion of own qualities
- ▶ Possessiveness: need to hold onto or control others or things
- ▶ Perfectionism: excessive need to get everything right

- ► False gratification: looking for comfort from wrong sources, e.g. food, sex, drinking
- ► Self-deception: "No one understands me"; false beliefs
- ► Fear of betrayal: unwillingness to trust anyone
- ► Unreality: withdrawal into fantasy world; avoidance of reality
- ► False responsibility: taking on inappropriate burdens
- ► Shyness: timidity; uneasiness or avoidance of other people.

6

The many causes of rejection

There are many reasons why rejection may come about, and they may affect us at any time, from the beginning of life. From these specific incidents the roots and fruits of rejection develop.

Conception and pregnancy

Rejection can begin in a wound or demonic oppression before a child is born. The enemy takes advantage of the most vulnerable. Many adults have found the source of their problems in earliest infancy or even earlier.

In *The Secret Life of the Unborn Child* (Verney and Kelly, Sphere Books, 1981), the authors state that "the unborn child is an aware, reacting human being who from the sixth month on (and perhaps earlier) leads an active emotional life." They add that "the fetus can see hear, experience, taste and, at a primitive level, even learn in *utero*. Most important, he can feel, not with an adult's sophistication, but feel nonetheless."

Verney and Kelly go on to say, "what a child feels and perceives begins shaping his attitudes and expectations about himself. Whether he ultimately sees himself (and hence acts) as an unhappy or sad, aggressive or meek, secure or anxiety-ridden person depends, in part, on the messages he gets about himself in the womb."

Therefore it is clear that a denial of love can affect a child before it is born. The womb is the child's first home. Is it friendly or unfriendly, peaceful or hostile? The child will receive both parents' feelings and thoughts. Their attitude and relationship with the baby before it is born will affect it after it is born.

The following are reasons for rejection before birth:

▶ Unwanted pregnancy, possibly because of conception too soon after marriage, too late in life, too large a family or financial problems

▶ Illegitimacy. Deuteronomy 23:2 speaks of a curse extending to ten generations. This can be cut off in Jesus' name

▶ Fear of deformity, or fear of childbirth

▶ Attempted abortion

▶ Pregnancy through rape, incest, adultery

▶ Drug or alcohol-dependent mothers

▶ Separation or divorce before the baby is born: often the child will take the blame

▶ Shock or trauma during pregnancy such as an accident or death of someone close.

We can be encouraged by many comforting words in Scripture. God is very concerned about children in the womb. The psalmist puts it very clearly:

> *For you created my inmost being;*
> *you knit me together in my mother's womb.*
> *I praise you because I am fearfully and wonderfully made;*
> *your works are wonderful,*
> *I know that full well.*
> *My frame was not hidden from you*
> *when I was made in the secret place.*
> *When I was woven together in the depths of the earth,*
> *your eyes saw my unformed body.*
> *All the days ordained for me*
> *were written in your book*
> *before one of them came to be.*   (Psalm 139:13–16)

Birth

It is clear that rejection can stem from the actual birth or soon afterwards. All these things can be factors:

▶ Pain, pressure, and loneliness of a long, protracted labor

▶ Difficult delivery, especially if instruments are used

▶ Emergency attention or surgery after birth requiring separation from the mother

▶ Congenital deformities

▶ The mother's death at the birth of the baby

▶ The baby being taken away for adoption

▶ Feeding problems interfering with mother-baby bonding

▶ Parents' own experience of rejection preventing them from showing love, acceptance and affection

▶ Parents wanting a boy instead of a girl, or vice versa, so that the child takes on guilt for being the "wrong" gender. This can be made worse if the couple is convinced that God told them the baby would be a different sex.

▶ The child not being named for a long time after the birth

▶ A child who was conceived as a "replacement" because an older sibling died

▶ Parents or doctors being unaware of a second baby in the womb.

Early childhood

Rejection can also affect a child as it is growing up. The first few months and years of a child's life are foundational and formative. Children mirror those who are close to them, and their spirits are wide open to receive both positive and negative things. The following factors may apply:

▶ Words such as "You were a mistake," "We didn't want any children," "We really wanted a boy/girl," "I wish you had never been born." Proverbs 18:21 says that *"Life and death is in the power of the tongue."*

▶ Separation too early in life or for too long, even for legitimate reasons

▶ Children given up for adoption or foster homes in their early years, even if they are later welcomed into a loving home

▶ Preferential treatment of one child over another, which may lead to attention-seeking and friction between siblings

▶ Early losses such as death, divorce, or separation

▶ Physical or mental disabilities, even speech impediments and the like

▶ Prolonged childhood illness or hospitalization

▶ Parents arguing or fighting in the family home, provoking insecurity, guilt and fear in the child.

School years

Rejection can occur in the very important years up to adulthood. The relationships between parents and children are key to a person's development. How we learn to view ourselves can affect us deeply. This may be affected by:

▶ Cruelty or domination by parents or older siblings

▶ Lack of affection and physical touch in the family

▶ Parents persistently ignoring the child

▶ Serious lack of communication in the family

▶ Negative comparison with other children in the family or at home

▶ Being sent to boarding school

▶ Being humiliated, severely punished or unfairly treated by teachers

▶ Bullying, exclusion from groups of friends, and name-calling

▶ Constant sickness causing academic problems

▶ Pressure from parents to succeed in school, leading to guilt and perfectionism

▶ Religious pressure and legalism

▶ Name-calling, emphasizing personal qualities or physical features

▶ Speech or learning difficulties such as stuttering and dyslexia

▶ Personal beliefs such as "I'm no good," "I'll never make it," "I'm too fat/thin/tall/short/ugly" etc., or "I want to be someone else"

▶ Lack of affirmation of a child's developing sexuality in adolescence.

Family circumstances

There is much that happens within the family and sometimes in outside circumstances that can cause rejection:

▶ Poverty or serious financial problems

▶ Long periods of unemployment

▶ A family member convicted of a crime

▶ Parents forcing their children into immoral or criminal behavior

▶ Sexual abuse, inside or outside the family

▶ Prematurely giving a child adult responsibilities

▶ Being evacuated or becoming a refugee in times of war

▶ A clinically depressed or mentally ill parent

▶ Alcoholism or other addictions in the family

▶ Shame or persecution about religious beliefs

▶ Unfaithfulness of parents, separation or divorce

▶ Ill-treatment by step-parents

▶ Premature death of a parent or other family member.

Later life

Well into adulthood, traumatic incidents can occur which create or highlight rejection issues:

▶ Guilt over a teenage pregnancy, sexual experience or abortion

▶ Failed love affairs

▶ Unwanted singleness

▶ Infertility

▶ Being disabled or having a major illness

▶ Serious problems with children

▶ Divorce, separation, or unfaithfulness of spouse

▶ Death of a marriage partner or other significant person.

All of these issues are important, and need to be considered sensitively. I would like to comment further on two of them.

Abuse

The incidence of abuse is now much more common, or commonly known. It can begin in the earliest years.

Verbal or mental abuse is any form of negative pressure by thoughts or words. Adults as well as children can be put down easily by words. Long silences can also be used manipulatively. Some people are persistently ignored when they talk, and that also is a form of rejection. Remember the power of the tongue for good and evil!

Physical abuse can affect children or marriage partners, or unmarried partners. The physical damage is bad enough, but there is also emotional hurt and humiliation which may take a long time to heal. There is a right and a wrong way to discipline children!

Sexual abuse is much more widely recognized than it was previously. The wounding it causes is a ready opening for demonic activity. The awareness of abuse is usually suppressed by the abuser, and its effects are buried deep within the person who has been victimized.

If abuse happens within the family, it engenders especially deep guilt, distrust, hatred and confusion. Children often endure the pain and shame because of loyalty or the fear of reprisals. The violation of their dignity, humanity and sexuality will bring problems in later life, especially in marital relationships. The person will grow up with a sense of defilement and inner conflict.

Abuse means betrayal, and it is always accompanied by feelings of rejection.

Broken marriages

Separation and or divorce of parents inevitably lead to some form of rejection. The rights and wrongs of the situation are not ultimately the issue. The spoken vows and the sexual act itself create a spiritual bond: as it is often declared at a church wedding, "Whom God has joined, let no one put asunder."

The tearing apart of separation and divorce causes deep wounding to the partners involved and also to the children. This can be particularly difficult for Christians, especially those in leadership. We need to be aware of the pain and rejection of being cast aside, the sense of worthlessness, as well as the loss of income, home, friends and school. For children it can mean losing the relationship with one, or even both parents.

Summary

It is clear that rejection can affect most if not every area of our lives. It is vital that we understand its emotional, social and spiritual impact so we can face it in the power of the Holy Spirit.

7

Jesus' experience of rejection

The key to the healing of rejection lies with Jesus. We need to consider how he identified with rejection from the very beginning of his life through to his death on the cross. It has been said that Jesus was the most rejected person who ever lived! Yet he never let rejection overcome or control him. He never manifested any of the fruit of rejection because the roots were never allowed to take hold.

Jesus suffered rejection but he did so in order to set us free from its grip. John sums up the rejection of Jesus:

> *He was in the world, and though the world was made through him, the world did not recognize him. He came to that which was his own, but his own did not receive him. Yet to all who received him, to those who believed in his name, he gave the right to become children of God.* (John 1:10–12)

Jesus' birth and early life

Luke 1:26–38 describes how Mary (likely as young as 16 years old) was greatly surprised and troubled by the appearance of an angel announcing that she would give birth to a baby by the Holy Spirit. The problem was that she was pledged to Joseph (Matthew 1:18–20), which under Jewish law was as serious a commitment as marriage. Mary could have been stoned as punishment for unfaithfulness.

In such a society, not much remained secret! Imagine the gossip, and the scandalous rumors. Joseph struggled with the news, planning to break the marriage contract because it was not his baby. It took an angel to convince him to marry Mary.

A census in the Roman world (Luke 2:1–5) meant that the family had to travel to their home town of Bethlehem to register. It was at least a three-day journey, very difficult for a pregnant woman. When they arrived at Bethlehem there was no accommodation for them, though it would seem likely that Joseph had family there – why could they not provide a room? Jesus was born in a cave-like stable with domestic animals.

This hardly sounds like the ideal start in life. But more sinister events were to come. King Herod, hearing from the magi that the Messiah was to be born, wanted to kill Jesus. He ordered a massacre of all the male children of two years old and under. The family fled to Egypt, where they remained until the ruthless king's death. They then returned to an obscure, poor town called Nazareth, where Joseph set up his carpentry business.

When Jesus was 12 years old, he accompanied his family to the temple in Jerusalem. A crisis occurred when Jesus went missing for three entire days. His parents finally found him in the temple with the teachers of the law (Luke 2:41–50). When Mary asked Jesus why he had treated them in such a way she was astonished and probably angry. They did not understand his reply: *"Didn't you know I had to be in my Father's house?"* Their lack of comprehension about his call must have added to the rejection Jesus had to deal with.

Jesus' ministry

Throughout the three-and-a-half years of Jesus' earthly ministry, he experienced much rejection. When crowds began to gather to hear him, his own family went to take charge of him, saying that he was out of his mind (Mark 3:21). John tells us that even his own brothers did not believe in him (John 7:5).

After Jesus spoke in the synagogue, people were so furious that they drove him out of town, trying to throw him over a cliff (Luke 4:28–30). Matthew records that Jesus' townspeople took offense at him, asking very cynically where a carpenter could get wisdom and miraculous powers. Jesus said to them, *"Only in their hometowns and in their own homes are prophets without honor"* (Matthew 13:57). Because of their unbelief (rejection), Jesus did not do very many miracles in that place.

Jesus' own people called him a Samaritan, which was a great insult for Jews in those days, and more than once said that he had a demon (John 7:20). He was criticized for eating with *"sinners"* – those who themselves were rejected from society – even though in so doing he brought them salvation (Luke 19:7).

When the religious leaders of the Jews felt they were losing their hold on the people, they began to plot against Jesus. They claimed that he was a blasphemer (Mark 2:6) because he talked about forgiving sins. They criticized him for eating with tax collectors and *"sinners"* (Mark 2:16) and for eating with *"unclean"* hands (Mark 7:5). It must have deeply grieved Jesus that they opposed the work of the God that he was doing.

The Pharisees announced that Jesus was possessed by Beelzebub, the prince of demons (Mark 3:22). They tried to test him by demanding miraculous signs (Mark 8:11, 12), challenging his authority (Mark 11:28) and asking difficult questions to try to catch him unawares (Mark 10:2–12, 12:13).

Jesus' trial and death

Jesus repeatedly foretold his coming rejection and death. He said,

> *The Son of Man must suffer many things and be rejected by the elders, chief priests and teachers of the law, and he must be killed.* (Luke 9:22)

> *The Son of Man is going to be betrayed into human hands.* (Luke 9:44)

> *But first he must suffer many things and be rejected by this generation.* (Luke 17:25)

> *He will be turned over to the Gentiles. They will mock him, insult him, spit on him, flog him and kill him.* (Luke 18:32)

Jesus' friends were so slow to understand, but after the resurrection they remembered his words (Luke 24:8).

Many of Jesus' own disciples had already turned back and no longer followed him because of his *"hard teachings."* He was betrayed by one of the Twelve, Judas (Luke 22:3–7, 47–48). When Jesus told the disciples that they would fall away, they refused to believe him (Matthew 26:35). Peter, although strongly vowing he would never disown Jesus, denied him three times (Luke 22:23).

At the time of Jesus' great trial, in the garden of Gethsemane, his friends fell asleep. He came to them three times in anguish and found them heavy with sleep each time (Mark 14:37–41). When an armed mob came to arrest him, everyone deserted him and fled (Mark 14:42–50).

After Jesus healed on the Sabbath, the Pharisees had begun to plot with the followers of Herod how they might kill him (Mark 3:6). The chief priests and the whole Sanhedrin looked for evidence against him, so that they could put him to death. Many people gave false testimony against him, although their statements disagreed (Mark 14:55–59).

Jesus suffered unspeakable physical pain as he was being crucified. There was also emotional torment, because he was continually mocked and insulted (Matthew 27:39; Mark 15:31). Yet the spiritual agony of the cross was even greater, because Jesus took our sin on himself, and that meant abandonment by his own Father.

The rejection of Jesus was made complete when the Father turned his back on his Son. Jesus cried out, *"My God, my God, why have you forsaken me?"*

Isaiah wrote:

He was despised and rejected by others,
a man of sorrows, and familiar with suffering.
Like one from whom people hide their faces,
he was despised, and we esteemed him not.
Surely he took up our infirmities
and carried our sorrows,
yet we considered him stricken by God,
smitten by him, and afflicted.
But he was pierced for our transgressions,
he was crushed for our iniquities;

> *the punishment that brought us peace was upon him,*
> *and by his wounds we are healed...*
> Yet it was the LORD's will to crush him
> *and cause him to suffer.*   (Isaiah 53:3–5, 10)

Why? It was all for love. Jesus' death and resurrection became a "divine exchange" for us. He took our rejection. In its place we can receive healing, acceptance, affirmation, love, security, and much more.

8

Dealing with rejection

We have just seen that God has dealt a death blow to rejection through his son Jesus. Yet there is a responsibility on our side too. We cannot be passive: we must take control over areas of rejection in our lives in the power of Jesus' name.

Obadiah prophesied:

> *On Mount Zion will be deliverance;*
> *it will be holy*
> *and the house of Jacob*
> *will possess its inheritance.* (Obadiah 17)

We need to take possession of what has been given to us in Christ!

Responsibility

We have a part to play in healing and wholeness. We must answer for our own attitudes and actions, even though the enemy may have got in or there is a hereditary factor. As we accept our personal accountability, healing will come within our grasp.

When Jesus began his ministry, he made this great pronouncement:

> *The Spirit of the Lord is on me,*
> *because he has anointed me*
> *to preach good news to the poor.*

> *He has sent me to proclaim freedom for the prisoners*
> *and recovery of sight for the blind,*
> *to release the oppressed,*
> *and to proclaim the year of the Lord's favor.*
>
> (Luke 4:18–19)

Then he said,

> *Today this scripture is fulfilled in your hearing.*   (Luke 4:21)

Although this was the prophetic fulfillment of God's will, it nevertheless required Jesus' willing participation. In the same way, we need to exercise our own faith for healing. Revelation demands a response.

The Father-heart of God

In the whole area of rejection it is essential that we recognize and understand the Father's heart. As we have already seen, many people's first experience of rejection has been through their earthly parents. Therefore they may worship God at a distance but feel unable to relate to him as a loving, caring Father.

The word *"Abba"* is used three times in the New Testament. As Jesus prayed in the garden of Gethsemane, he called his Father *"Abba."* This is the same everyday word used in Jewish culture for a child to speak to his daddy. It is a warm and familiar yet respectful term for father, used also by adult sons and daughters. Yet for Jesus to speak to God in that way was ground-breaking.

This same word is taken up in Romans 8:15 and Galatians 4:6 by the church. We too can express our love and requests to the Father by saying to him, "Abba." We have been adopted into the family of God and he says to us,

> *I will be a Father to you,*
> *and you will be my sons and daughters.*
>
> (2 Corinthians 6:18)

God knows that rejection is a barrier between us. As the great Father, his desire is that we have security, peace, emotional stability, affirmation and acceptance. Just as he spoke to Jesus, *"You are my son, whom I love; with you I am well pleased"* (Luke 3:21), he also speaks to us.

Our identity is found in relationships. We need to come into a real relationship with God as our Father, receive his acceptance of us, and then move into accepting ourselves and others.

But first we may have to acknowledge the things that may be a barrier.

Disappointment

Disappointment can hinder any response to God's healing presence. Proverbs 13:12 says that *"hope deferred makes the heart sick."* When our deep longings for affection and acceptance have not been met, our frustration and hurt can prevent us from reaching out in faith and trust. This too can become a foothold for the enemy.

Shame

The experience of being rejected often leaves a sense of humiliation or shame. The enemy will try to take advantage by accusing us and condemning us, which can easily lead to self-rejection and withdrawal. Yet however painful past events have been, they must be faced with the grace of God. Often as we speak out our confession in the presence of others, the stronghold of shame is broken.

Forgiveness

Whenever there are wounds of rejection, there are people to forgive. We need to look honestly at our feelings towards those who have hurt us, bringing them into the light of God. This may involve confessing our feelings about God. We may well have to forgive ourselves, too.

A parable that Jesus told shows up the issue of unforgiveness in a very clear light. A servant who himself had been forgiven a great debt would not forgive others. Therefore he was sentenced to torment in prison, until he paid his own debt (Matthew

18:21–35). Someone has said, "The one who cannot forgive others breaks the bridge over which he must pass himself, for every person has to be forgiven."

We too have already been forgiven a debt so big we could never have paid it on our own. The amount far exceeds anything that another person may owe us. In Jesus' story, the master was motivated by mercy and generosity, but his anger flared when he saw the servant's own unwillingness to forgive.

Unforgiveness is sin and will be judged by God, no matter what has happened to us. It imprisons and tortures the one who cannot forgive, and can create an entrance for demonic powers. It becomes a barrier to our relationship with others and with God.

In Ephesians 2:14, Paul says that Jesus has *"destroyed the barrier, the dividing wall of hostility."* Through his own body he reconciled us to God and with each other. Colossians 2:13–14 tells us that Jesus forgave us all our sins, canceling the written code against us by nailing it on the cross. If a barrier still remains, it is on our side, not God's. And if we refuse to forgive, we are nullifying Jesus' sacrifice.

Forgiveness may need to be a process. How long? We have to keep forgiving until the pain goes. We have to keep forgiving until we begin to see the other person differently, to speak of them and to them differently, and to no longer strive to get even. True forgiveness will alter our relationship with the person who has offended us. It will free us to bless and be blessed.

Repentance of sin

Is repentance necessary with rejection? Yes! Rejection is completely bound up with sin. It leads us to sin against ourselves, others, and the One who created us. The wrong reactions we have to sins against us can cause us to commit those same sins with others.

We often make repentance too cheap – a quick prayer. Yet it is a costly issue. It is a change of heart, will, thinking and emotions. It is deliberately turning away from sin and turning to God with a change of lifestyle.

Look at the way David repented in Psalm 51. He responded clearly and completely to the word of God. He fully confessed his own guilt and laid it before God, crying out for forgiveness. Because of this he was not tormented forever by his sin but was able to make a clean break from it.

Paul gives us a key to repentance in 2 Corinthians 7:8–11. He commends the Corinthians for expressing sorrow that led them to repentance.

> *Godly sorrow brings repentance that leads to salvation and leaves no regret, but worldly sorrow brings death. See what this godly sorrow has produced in you: what earnestness, what eagerness to clear yourselves, what indignation, what alarm, what longing, what concern, what readiness to see justice done.*
> (2 Corinthians 7:10–11)

We need to acknowledge the pain in repentance and also the fact that it takes time, commitment and emotional energy.

In Acts 2:37–38, we read that the people who heard the word of God were *"cut to the heart and said to Peter and the other apostles 'Brothers, what shall we do?'"* Peter called them all to repent. We also need to let our hearts be penetrated by the word of God and respond accordingly. It is then that repentance becomes effective.

Inner healing

Those things that have been fed into our emotional memories do not disappear with time. Negative input will remain to cause us harm unless we can receive inner healing.

Hebrews 13:8 tells us *"Jesus Christ is the same yesterday and today and forever."* Jesus is not limited by our time and space. He is outside of it, yet breaks into it through the Holy Spirit. He is fully capable of healing yesterday's problems and hurts today.

Someone has said that "Inner healing is a ladder, not a single rung; a process, rarely a one-time event." Those of us who counsel and pray for healing must bear that in mind. In the pressure to get things sorted out, it is easy to be insensitive. It may be good to prepare for a time of ministry by fasting or reading specific scriptures.

In inner healing we need to acknowledge the hurts and wounded memories and surrender them to Jesus, asking the Holy Spirit to bring healing. We must allow a release of emotion – letting it happen without pushing the feelings of pain down.

In the case of rejection, often deliverance is needed along with inner healing. The ability to distinguish between spirits is a gift of the Holy Spirit (1 Corinthians 12:10). We need to be able to discern what is from God, what is from ourselves, and what is demonic – sometimes it's not easy!

If you are clear that there is some demonic intrusion, take authority in prayer and cast out the demon, being as specific as possible. If there is a struggle with a manifestation of some kind, press through. There may need to be more than one session. Finally, ask the Holy Spirit to fill the empty place with God's presence (Luke 11:14–26).

Finally, broken relationships can be restored. Because we have been reconciled to God through the cross, we can be reconciled to each other. In place of enmity there can be friendship. As deep wounds are healed, trust can be restored, and the peace of God can rule again in place of fear.

As we come out of rejection, breaking the bread of Holy Communion can be an appropriate response. Jesus said, *"Do this in remembrance of me."* Our new-found acceptance can be considered in the light of the cross. Jesus died and then rose from the dead so that we could live in freedom and relationship with God. Identity, security and esteem are all part of what we receive from Jesus' broken body.

9

Moving on from rejection

Who would have chosen a failure like Peter to preach on the day of Pentecost? After vowing never to leave Jesus, he denied him with oaths and curses. No wonder he went away weeping bitterly (Luke 22:54–62). He returned to his old job, no longer considered one of the disciples.

Yet Jesus appeared at the lakeside and confronted Peter, challenging him three times, once for every time Peter had denied him (John 21:15–19). Through this persistence, Peter's identity, direction and role were restored. He was healed from the past and given purpose for the future.

Many of us can identify with Peter's sense of failure and self-rejection. We need the restoration he received, as well as the discipling that came with it.

It is important that pastoral care follows prayer for deliverance and healing. After deep ministry, it may not be easy for people to just carry on in isolation. The church needs to disciple believers, and those who have received prayer must be willing to be discipled. Through practicing these basic disciplines of the faith, we can grow out of rejection and into maturity.

Maintaining healing

After a time of prayer, it is necessary to press forward in healing. We all need good, honest relationships where it is possible to talk and pray things through on an ongoing basis. Some people feel disoriented for a while after prayer for healing and deliverance. Good and consistent communication is important for accountability.

Therefore it is helpful to plan times to assess progress. If the person who prayed originally is not able to continue contact, find someone else in the local church to do follow-up. In this way the growth and healing can continue.

The following areas of discipleship must all be considered:

1. *Spiritual knowledge*: Understanding the power of the cross and the crucified life is vital in the ongoing warfare with the flesh and demonic powers.

2. *Scripture*: Reading, applying and living from the word of God is essential to keep our freedom in Jesus.

3. *Prayer and praise*: Thanking and worshiping God for his work of release is part of the process of growth.

4. *Renewing the mind*: Exercising self-control in the area of emotions, thoughts, and will is important to prevent the enemy from further attack.

5. *Positive confession*: 1 Corinthians 14:3 tells us to strengthen, encourage, and build up one another with our speech.

6. *The Father-heart of God*: Each person must learn to relate to God as a loving Father.

7. *Healthy sexuality*: Often there are identity issues to do with masculinity and femininity that must be worked out.

8. *Confidence and self-esteem*: Self-worth and value that has been undermined by rejection must be restored.

9. *The body of Christ*: Both giving and receiving in the local church is part of growth and maturity.

10. *Submission and resisting*: James 4:7 tells us to resist the enemy and submit to God – relating rightly to authority.

11. *Laughter*: Nehemiah 8:10 tells us that the joy of the Lord is our strength!

As we trust the Holy Spirit to guide us, and others to support us, we will grow in our walk with Jesus. We must learn to live in the opposite spirit to rejection. Yes, there will be failure, but in Christ we can learn to overcome. God wants all of his children to know his acceptance, forgiveness, affirmation and blessing.

Appendix

Family history questionnaire

In counseling, I have found it very helpful to ask a series of questions relating to the counselee's history. This method saves time while clearly pinpointing specific issues for follow-up. I often give out the questionnaire a week or two in advance, which allows time for the questions to be answered honestly and thoughtfully.

Going through these questions will open up issues of a person's life that will be important in their healing. We need to trust the Holy Spirit to bring the most pertinent issues to the forefront. The object is to look at the person's history from conception right through to where they are today.

1. What is your first memory?
2. Were you wanted?
3. Were you illegitimate?
4. Was there any attempted abortion?
5. Did your birth follow a miscarriage or stillbirth?
6. Did your parents want a child of a different sex?
7. Was the birth traumatic?
8. Were you and your mother able to bond together?
9. Who brought you up?
10. How well do you know your father?

11. Was he away much during your childhood?

12. Did you receive affectionate hugs and kisses from your parents?

13. Who disciplined you, and how?

14. Did your parents take time to listen to you?

15. Can you remember any of your parents turning away when you needed help?

16. How did you try to get attention from your parents?

17. What is your unhappiest memory?

18. Who was the dominant force in your home?

19. Was anyone "always right" in your family?

20. How did your parents relate to each other?

21. Are your parents still together, and how do they relate now?

22. If there was separation or divorce, what do you remember about it?

23. Whose lap would you sit on?

24. What was your order of birth?

25. Were there favorites in your family?

26. Did you relate well to your brothers/sisters?

27. Did you like school? What are your memories?

28. Did you go to a boarding school? At what age?

29. Was there legalism or religious pressure in your home?

30. Can you remember any negative words that were applied to you?

31. Do you like yourself?

32. Do you dislike or feel threatened by men?

33. Do you dislike or feel threatened by women?

34. Do you eat regularly? Were there unusual eating habits in your family?

35. Have you ever thought about an overdose or suicide?

36. Do you have troubled sleep or nightmares? What are they?

37. Do you have sexual difficulties or a troubled thought-life?

38. How did you learn about sex, and from whom?

39. Have you engaged in sex outside of marriage?

40. Was there any inappropriate sexual attention or abuse when you were growing up?

41. Did you experience any physical or mental abuse?

42. Do you have strange feelings towards people of the same sex?

43. Have you been used for lust (money, sex, power) rather than loved for yourself?

44. Do you struggle with feelings of shame?

45. Do you struggle with guilt feelings? If so, what for?

46. Have you experienced great disappointment or been let down and betrayed?

47. Is there anyone you have difficulty forgiving?

48. Do you have any habits you cannot control?

49. Are you afraid of anyone or anything?

50. If you are married, have you felt dominated by your partner?

51. Have you experienced separation or divorce?

52. Do you feel used and abused in your marriage?

53. Are you a single parent? Has that led to hurt and rejection?

54. Do you feel discarded by the church, or have difficulty making relationships in the church?

55. How do you relate to authority figures, including church leaders?

56. Have you been unemployed?

57. Have you experienced rejection in your workplace or in applying for jobs?

58. Is there any Freemasonry in your family or ancestry?

59. Is there any family involvement in superstition, spiritism, séances, magic, faith healing, tarot cards, ouija boards or other occult practices?

60. Have you been hypnotized?

61. Have you been involved in any of the martial arts, yoga, or TM?

62. Do you feel you have failed God?

63. Do you long for affection and love?

64. Do you find it hard to express emotions? What happens to them?

65. Do your emotions come out in an explosion or do they hurt you inside?

66. Do you weep very much? Are there particular reasons why?

67. Do you find it difficult to communicate what you're thinking and feeling?

68. What kind of a relationship do you have with your own children?

69. Do you find it difficult to affirm them?

70. Do you frequently criticize your children?

71. Do you love your family with actions or words?

72. Do you know God's affirmation or do you hear, "Do more"?

73. Do you say positive things to other people?

74. Do you say what other people want to hear in order to please them?

75. Do you feel the need to justify yourself or defend yourself from attack?

76. Do you have difficulty trusting people; are you afraid of being taken advantage of?

77. Do you find it difficult to apologize when you've done something wrong?

78. Do you think that if people knew your failings they would reject or abandon you?

79. Has God ever said to you, "You're forgiven"?

80. Is God your *"Abba"* (Romans 8:15)?

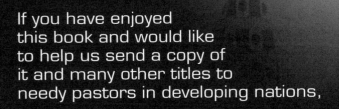

If you have enjoyed
this book and would like
to help us send a copy of
it and many other titles to
needy pastors in developing nations,

please write for further information,
or send your gift to:

Sovereign World Trust
PO Box 777
Tonbridge
Kent TN11 OZS
United Kingdom

www.sovereignworldtrust.com.